CW01510151

Easy Indian Veg Recipes

Taste of North & South India

Contents

Cooking for first time? Nervous, where to start?
Want good tips to impress your family?

Hey Newbies!
Don't worry, this collection of recipes is just right for 'You'
Get started with some easy and quick to make North and South Indian dishes, with ingredients found in every kitchen. Cooking is an art; you can learn by doing and combining the different flavours in your own unique way with lots of Love.

Who Am I?
Another newbie who started going into the kitchen after marriage for real cooking and not just to make tea. And when its North meets South, the challenge is more exciting.
These are not just recipes, they are stories from my home experts' mother & mother-in-law, of their cooking us delicious meals all these years. Now they are very much part of my kitchen.
Here in this collection, I am presenting you with few recipes from North and South India that are a little hatke yet simple to prepare. I have also put down some useful tips that I learnt along the way.

Enjoy and Have Fun!!
Manisha Nigam

Recipe 01 : Mother's Mango Chutney - Good For Summers

Onset of summers and the first thing comes to mind is Mangos and the yummy chutney that our mothers make. It is not only tasty but a good summer cooler. Mango, the king of fruits has many health benefits too; it contains good balance of water and fibrous contents, antioxidants, Vitamin A, B and C and has minerals such as potassium, magnesium and iron. As it is said, everything in limits is good. Have even heard few doctors advising patients, including diabetics, to take seasonal fruits like Mangos but in limit. So how to make it easily at home. Here it is...

ITEMS NEEDED
(tsp: teaspoon, tbs: tablespoon, gm: grams, kg: kilo grams, cup: approx. 250ml)

1. Kacha Aam (Raw Mango) – 1 Kg
2. Namak (Salt) - 1 tsp
3. Desi Ghee (Clarified butter) - 1 tsp
4. Lal Mirch powder (Red Chili powder) - 1 tsp
5. Saunf Powder (Aniseed, Fennel Seed) - 1 tsp
6. Garam Masala (Mixture of ground spices) - 1 tsp
7. Sonth Powder (Dry Ginger powder) - 1 tsp
8. Cheeni (Sugar) - 200 gm
9. Saphed Sirka (White Vinegar) (optional) – ¼ tsp

PREPARATION
First, clean, peel and grate the mangos.

Heat a cooking pan and add grated mangos with salt. Cover it with a lid and let it cook for around 2-3 mins. till the mangos get a little soft.

Now add desi ghee and stir for 1min.

Then add red chilli, saunf, garam masala, sonth powder and stir for another 1 min.

Note: In case you don't have ready-made garam masala at home, you can easily make it at home. See Garam Masala recipe.

Mix sugar in the mango pulp and stir continuously until sugar melts.

Take it off the flame and let it cool down. Store it in a jar, glass jar is preferred. You can also add white vinegar, which will work as a preservative.

This chutney will stay good for more than a week.

Recipe 02 :   Simple Nariyal Chutney - Enjoy With Idli, Dosa Etc.

Nariyal or coconut chutney is every south Indian home's recipe. It is a side dish that is served with idli, dosa, vada, uttapam, pongal etc. The chutney ingredients like coconut, ginger, green chilies are very beneficial for health. Coconut has saturated fats, high fibre contents, ginger is good for congestion, cold, sore throat etc and green chilli has antioxidant, Vitamin C. Recipe here, is one which I learnt from my mother-in-law and now I can proudly say I am good at it.

ITEMS NEEDED
(tsp: teaspoon, tbs: tablespoon, gm: grams, kg: kilo grams, cup: approx.. 250ml)

1.   Grated Nariyal (Coconut) – ¼ cup
2.   Bhuna Chana (Fried / Roasted Gram) – ¼ cup
3.   Hari Mirch (Green Chili) – 4-5 medium size
4.   Adrak (Ginger) – 4-5 small pieces of approx. 1cm
5.   Imli (Tamarind) / Amchur Powder (Dry mango powder) – 1tsp
6.   Namak (Salt) – 1tsp
7.   Paani (Water) – ¼ cup, add more if required
8.   Til ka Tel (Sesame / Gingili oil) – 1 tsp, or any other oil of your choice
9.   Kala Sarson (Black Mustard seeds) – ½ tsp
10. Sukhi Lal Mirch (Dried Red Chili) – 1 small size
11. Urad Dal (white gram) – ¼ tsp
12. Kadi Patta (Curry Leaves) – 2-3 leaves

PREPARATION

In a grinder add the grated nariyal, bhuna chana, green chillies, imli, adrak, salt and water. Grind it well, not too coarse nor fine, just medium consistency. Add additional water if required and salt as per taste. Empty the contents, the chutney in a bowl.

Instead of grated nariyal you can also use small pieces of nariyal that can be grounded easily. Use fresh nariyal for a better taste.

In my house we use bhuna chana, it gives a good texture and nutty aroma to the chutney. You can make the chutney wholly with nariyal as well.

In a small pan to make the tadka, heat the oil well and then add kala sarson. Let it crackle and then add urad dal, keep it till it becomes light brown. Then add the curry leaves and let them become crisp.
Now pour the contents to the chutney in the bowl.

You could also add dried red chilli in the tadka if you want it to be hotter.

Chutney is ready!!

Tip: Nariyal has saturated fats that may not suit some people. Don't worry, don't avoid the chutney as you can easily reduce it by soaking the grated nariyal or nariyal pieces in water for 2-3 mins before using it. Drain the water and then use the nariyal for making chutney.

Recipe 03 : Gun Powder - South India's Hot Chutney

Don't get scared, it is not real gun powder. It is south India's favourite hot chutney, good one to have with idli, dosa, upma or any other food like cheelas, khichdi where you need a hot chutney. Easy to prepare and can be stored for many days.

ITEMS NEEDED
(tsp: teaspoon, tbs: tablespoon, gm: grams, kg: kilo grams, cup: approx. 250ml)

1. Chana dal (Split chickpeas) - 1 cup
2. Urad dal (white gram) - 1 cup
3. Lal Mirch (Red chili) - 7-8 medium size
4. Safed Til (White Sesame seeds) – ¼ cup
5. Oil – 2 tbs

PREPARATION
Dry roast the white til.

Take oil in a pan. Add chana dal, urad dal and mirch to it. Fry them till urad dal becomes a little brown.

Pour the contents in a container or plate. Add the white til and mix it well.

Let them cool down. Then grind the mixture into a nice powder. It could be a little coarse for crunchy taste. Store this mixture in an air tight container.

When you want to use, take the required amount of powder (1-2 tsp) and pour ¼ tsp of edible oil to make a paste.

Recipe 04 : Prepare Dosa & Idli – Completely At Home

Dosa and Idli are the most famous dishes of south, loved by north as well. Getting the right batter is the key for preparing soft, spongy idlis and nice crunchy dosas. No worries, no need to buy batter from market or ready mix for dosa and idli when you can easily prepare it at home. The ingredients, their ratio and proper consistency are the key for making a good batter and here I am sharing what I learned from my mother-in-law. Prepare the batter and make delicious dosas and idlis.

ITEMS NEEDED
(tsp: teaspoon, tbs: tablespoon, gm: grams, kg: kilo grams, cup: approx. 250ml)

This will make around 10-12 medium size dosas.
1. Urad dal (white gram) – 1 cup
2. Special South Chawal (Idli Rice) – 3-4 cups
3. Namak (Salt) – 1tbs
4. Tel (Oil) – ¼ cup

PREPARATION

Making the Batter …
I will first start with the ratio, in case there is a confusion. For dosa, ratio should be 1:4 i.e., take 1 cup of Urad dal and 4 cups of Rice. And for idli mix ratio should be 1:3.

Best batter is made of the special south Indian rice that is called Idli rice or boiled rice, that you can get easily from any South Indian shop. This variety of rice is fat, petite or short-grained and parboiled.

Soak the dal and rice in water, in separate containers for few hours before grinding. Duration depends on the weather conditions, minimum 5-6 hrs will give you good results.

Clean the soaked dal and rice nicely with fresh water. Drain all the water once done.

Put urad dal in the mixer with half a cup of water and grind it well. Add water if required so that no solid dal particles remain. The batter should be moderately thick with smooth consistency.

Now grind the rice with water, again with enough so that it is easily grounded. For dosa the rice should be grinded very fine and for idli it should be a little coarse like sooji (semolina / granulated wheat).

Mix the grounded dal and rice together, your hand is the best tool here that I prefer, in a container with enough room to allow it to rise. Add salt, mix it well and leave it for another 5-6 hrs.

You should be good to go!

Tip: You can check if urad dal has grinded well by taking some water in a cup and drop a little batter in water (like a small drop). If it is done well, it will immediately come on surface of the water.
If the weather is warm (say, above 20 deg. Celsius / 70 deg. Fahrenheit), the batter will easily ferment when left on the countertop. If it is cold, put the batter inside the oven or microwave. Another way is to warm the oven or microwave a little, turn it off, and then place the batter container inside to ferment.

Your batter is ready, Now make Idli and Dosa ...

For Idli, grease the idli stand with little oil and then pour the batter. Fill it just below the top rim such that when cooked the idli gets space to rise. Duration for cooking will depend on your idli maker or stand that you are using. In case you are not sure, keep it on medium flame for 7-8 mins and check if nicely cooked. Else keep it for another 5-6mins.

Tip: To check if idli is cooked well, sprinkle little water over the idli and prick it with your finger. If your finger comes out clean then your idli is done.

For Dosa, grease the dosa tawa or pan (a flat heavy tawa is best) with little oil spread evenly. When sufficiently hot, spread the dosa batter evenly in a round or oval shape. You can use a katori (small cup) or a serving spoon or ladle, whichever is easier. Pour little oil around the dosa and little over it spreading across. Cook nicely from both sides till it is crispy.

Tip: Cut an onion into two halves and rub the cut side on the dosa tawa for cleaning it after making each dosa. This will make sure that the tawa is clean and smooth for use. Then, you can skip greasing the tawa with oil every time before pouring the batter.

Recipe 05 :   Adai Dosa – A Filling Breakfast

Adai dosa is a south indian savoury pan cake made of lentils, rice and spices. It is protein rich, healthy and a good morning breakfast. Enjoy it with coconut chutney or gun powder or dahi (curd).

ITEMS NEEDED
(tsp: teaspoon, tbs: tablespoon, gm: grams, kg: kilo grams, cup: approx. 250ml)

This will make around 7-8 medium size adai dosas.
1. Urad Dal (White Gram) – ½ cup
2. Channa Dal (Split chickpeas) – ½ cup
3. Arhar or Toor Dal (Split pigeon peas) – ½ cup
4. Lobiya (Black Eyed pea)– ½ cup
5. Moong Dal (Green Gram) – ½ cup
6. Special South Chawal (Idli Rice) – 2½ cups
7. Lal Mirch (Red chili) – 6-8
8. Kali Mirch (Black Pepper) – 6-8
9. Namak (Salt) – 2-3 tbs

PREPARATION
Soak all the dals urad, channa, arhar, lobiya, moong & rice for 3-4 hrs. You can soak all the dals together and preferably rice separately in a container.

Wash the rice and grind it into a fine mixture with water.

Wash the soaked dals and grind them with lal mirch, kali mirch and water into a coarse mixture. We need a little thick batter so make sure it is not too watery.

Mix the two mixtures well (I prefer doing with my hand, best tool), add salt and leave it for another 2-3 hrs.

The mixture will rise a little after sometime. Check the batter and add more salt if required and mix well. If the batter has become too thick, add some water. It should be of thick flowing consistency. Mix well after adding water and salt.

Add a pinch of hing (asafoetida), it helps in digestion.
You can also add finely grated coconut in the mixture.

And when it is ready to make, heat a tawa or pan. Brush little oil evenly on the tawa and spread the adai dosa mixture in an oval shape.
Make a tiny oval shape in the centre of your dosa by removing the batter from there, in order to pour some oil in between. This will help in cooking it well from the centre. Also pour oil around the dosa and cook it on medium flame from both sides.

Adai dosa is a little thicker than usual rice dosa, add additional oil if required so that it gets a good brownish colour.
Serve it hot with chutney or dahi.

Tip: For instant use, add sour yogurt in the mixture and make adai dosas.
To give it a north touch, you can add finely chopped pyaaz (onions) and hara dhaniya (coriander leaves), adrak (ginger) paste, jeera (cumin seeds) in the batter before making the dosas.

Recipe 06 : Hatke Kadhi - A South Style Preparation

Kadhi is very popular among people in north India. It is made in south India also but the preparation is a little different. I am going to give you a recipe of a hatke kadhi, a different south Indian style of preparation.

ITEMS NEEDED
(tsp: teaspoon, tbs: tablespoon, gm: grams, kg: kilo grams, cup: approx. 250ml)

1. Dahi (Curd) - 500 ml
2. Tinda (Apple Gourd) – 2 medium size
3. Chana dal (Split chickpeas) – ¼ cup
4. Fresh Grated Nariyal (Coconut) – ¼ cup
5. Hari Mirch (Green Chillies) - 5-6 medium size
6. Kala Sarson (Black Mustard Seeds) - 2 tbs
7. Zeera (Cumin Seeds) - 1 tbs
8. Sukhi Lal Mirch (Dry Red Chilli) - 2-3 pieces
9. Namak (Salt) - 3-4 tbs (as per taste)
10. Kadi Patta (Curry leaves) – 10-12 leaves
11. Ghee or Oil - 1-2 tbs
12. Urad Dal (white gram) – ¼ tsp

PREPARATION
Soak the chana dal in water for 10-15 mins.

Cut the tinda in small pieces, say 8-10 parts of each. Boil the tinda pieces in small amount of water till they are almost 90% soft. I used tinda as it's a good combination, you can also use bottle gourd or ghiya or even make it without if you want to keep it simple.

Make a paste in mixer of soaked chana dal, nariyal, green chilli, kala sarson, zeera. Add a little water so that the paste is smooth.

Beat the curd to make it smooth.

In a pan or kadhai or deep cooking pot, put the boiled tinda, dahi, paste, curry patta and mix it well. Keep it on medium flame till it boils nicely and the tinda is fully cooked.

Now prepare the tadka. In a small tadka pan heat ghee or oil nicely, add sarson and let it crackle. Then add urad dal and let it be a little brown. At last add the red chillies and after they are fried, put the tadka in the kadhi.

Tip: A little sour curd makes a good kadhi. You can also add pakoda in the kadhi or make it as a side dish to spice it up.

Recipe 07 : Sambhar With Saijan Ki Phalli

Sambhar is one of the essential dishes in a South Indian meal. It is easy and fast to make. It is a common dish, hence over the years it has evolved and people have innovated their own styles of making it. Here I will give you mine that I learned and have been making now successfully, keeping my family happy with the taste.

The main ingredient is a good Sambhar powder. I prefer to make it at home, then the taste is all in my hands. See the Sambhar Powder recipe for making it at home.

ITEMS NEEDED
(tsp: teaspoon, tbs: tablespoon, gm: grams, kg: kilo grams, cup: approx. 250ml)

1. Sambhar Powder – 3 tsp (see Sambhar Powder recipe or use ready-made available in market)
2. Methi dana powder (Fenugreek powder) – ½ tsp (may not require with ready-made sambhar powder)
3. Saijan ki phalli (Drumsticks)* – 1 stick
4. Arhar or Toor dal (Slit pigeon peas) – ¼ cup
5. Amchoor powder (Dry mango powder)** - 2 tsp
6. Hari Mirch (Green Chili) – 2=3 medium size
7. Adrak (Ginger) – ½ tsp (grated or finely chopped)
8. Namak (Salt) – 2 tsp
9. Haldi (Turmeric powder) – ½ tsp
10. Hing (Asafoetida) – ¼ tsp
11. Sukhi Lal Mirch (Red chili) – 2 medium size
12. Kala Sarson (Black Mustard seeds) – ½ tsp
13. Urad dal (white gram) – ¼ tsp
14. Tel (oil) – 1 tsp
15. Kadi Patta (Currey Leaves) – 1 stem
16. Paani (Water) – 2-3 cups

You can use other vegetables as well instead like Chote pyaaz (baby onions), Gajar (Carrot), Mooli (Raddish), Baigan (Brinjal), Ghiya or Lauki (Bottle Gourd), Karela (Bitter Gourd) and make different variety of sambhar.

** You can also use Imli (Tamarind). Soak handful (1/2 tbs) of tamarind in water (1/4 cup) for 15-20 mins. Squeeze the tamarind to get the pulp, strain and use.

PREPARATION

Wash, peel and cut the saijan ki phali (drumsticks) into pieces of around 2 inches in length. Boil the phalli in water on medium flame till they are just soft. Not too soft as they will again get cooked in the sambhar.

Wash the dal and boil it with water till it is soft. You can either do it in a cooker, 4 whistles will be enough. Can also boil in a covered kadai or pan but that will take longer, 10-15 mins more depending on the quality of the dal.

Take the pan or kadai or any other utensil in which you want to cook the sambhar. Put the dal and phali, along with the water in which you had boiled the dal and phali. Add additional water if required.

Add green chilis along with the grated or finely chopped ginger, kadi patta, sambhar powder, namak, haldi, amchoor powder and hing.

Cook the sambhar on a medium flame for around 10 mins, let it boil nicely so that masalas or all spices get mixed well and the phali are soft.

In parallel prepare the tadka to be put in the sambhar. Heat the oil in tadka pan and when hot add the kala sarson. Let it crackle and then add the urad dal and sukhi lal mirch pieces. Fry them nicely and then put the tadka in the prepared Sambhar.

Tip: To make the consistency of sambhar thick, you can add either wheat flour or rice flour. Add the flour slowly while constantly mixing it well so that no lumps are formed. Then give it a boil for 1 min.

Recipe 08 :   Kali Mirch Lahsun Rasam

Rasam is a must for lunch and dinner in most of the south Indian houses. North Indians see it as a variety of soup and is also in soup category in menu cards. Rasam is not only tasty but has health benefits too, is good for digestion. This recipe is very good for winters as it has lot of kali mirch and lahsun.

ITEMS NEEDED
(tsp: teaspoon, tbs: tablespoon, gm: grams, kg: kilo grams, cup: approx. 250ml)

1. Rasam / Sambhar Powder – 1 tsp (see Rasam Powder recipe or use ready-made available in market)
2. Kali Mirch (Black Pepper) – 10-12 pieces / 2 tsp
3. Lahsun (Garlic) – 5-6 cloves (peeled)
4. Amchoor powder (Dry mango powder)** - 3-4 tsp
5. Namak (Salt) – 2 tsp
6. Haldi (Turmeric powder) – ½ tsp
7. Hing (Asafoetida) – ¼ tsp
8. Sukhi Lal Mirch (Red chili) – 2 medium size
9. Kala Sarson (Black Mustard seeds) – ½ tsp
10. Ghee (Clarified butter) – 1-2 tsp
11. Kadi Patta (Currey Leaves) – 1 stem or 7-8 leaves
12. Hara Dhaniya (Coriander Leaves) – 1-2 stems (chopped leaves)
13. Paani (Water) – 2-3 cups

** You can also use Imli (Tamarind). Soak handful (1/2 tbs) of tamarind in water (1/4 cup) for 15-20 mins. Squeeze the tamarind to get the pulp, strain and use.

PREPARATION
Heat the ghee in kadai or pan and add kala sarson and let it crackle.

Then add hing, lal mirch (broken into 2-3 pieces each) and fry till lal mirch changes colour.

Now add the main ingredients, lahsun and kali mirch, and fry till lahsun is brown and soft. You can also use crushed kali mirch instead of whole.

Then add water, rasam powder, namak, haldi, kadi patta, amchoor powder or imli pulp and mix well. Let the rasam cook for 10-15 mins on low flame.

At the end add chopped hara dhaniya leaves and boil for another 1 min.

Your rasam is ready!

Recipe 09 :   Bhindi (Lady's Finger) Gojju Recipe

Gojju is curry Andhra style. This recipe uses bindi or lady's finger and imli as the main ingredients. You can think of it as sambhar without dal.

ITEMS NEEDED
(tsp: teaspoon, tbs: tablespoon, gm: grams, kg: kilo grams, cup: approx. 250ml)

1. Bhindi (Lady's Finder) – 6-7 pieces
2. Hari Mirch (Green Chilli) – 4-5 medium size
3. Imli (Tamarind) – 1 cup
4. Kala Sarson (Black Mustard Seeds) – 1 tsp
5. Tel (Oil) – 1-2 tbs
6. Urad dal (White gram) – ¼ tsp
7. Kadi Patta (Curry Leaves) – 8-10 leaves
8. Sambhar Powder – 1-2 tbs
9. Methi dana powder (Fenugreek powder) – ½ tsp (may not require with ready-made sambhar powder)
10. Haldi (Turmeric) – ¼ tsp
11. Namak (Salt) – 1 tsp
12. Paani (Water) – 2 cups

PREPARATION
Cut the bhindi into small pieces, around 1 inch. Cut the green chilis length wise into two halves.

Soak handful of imli in water and keep it aside. Luke warm water will be better. Make good quantity as we will use imli water as base for the recipe.

In a pan or kadhai or deep cooking pot, heat the oil well and add kala sarson, let it crackle. Add urad dal, once it is brown add green chilis and bhindi. Keep it on low flame till bhindi is a little soft. You don't want it to be too soft as it is going to boil with imli water later.

Now add the imli water, see that it is as per your taste and not too sour. Add additional water if required. Put the curry leaves, sambhar powder, methi powder, turmeric and salt. Adjust the amount of salt as per your taste. Keep it on medium flame and let it boil for ~10-15mins, till your bhindi is soft enough.

You can use sambhar powder that is available in the market or you can make it at home. See the Sambhar powder recipe.

You are done ... Enjoy!

Tip: This recipe can also be made with karela (bitter gourd) or baingan (brinjal) or gajar (carrot). In order to get consistency, you can add little aata (whaet or rice flour) while stirring so that lumps are not there.

Recipe 10 :   Ragi (Finger Millet) Cheela

Cheela is a very popular dish for breakfast and as evening snack. In north India besan (gram or chick pea flour) cheela and dal cheela are very popular. We will make another variety of cheela, Ragi cheela. It is not very common but it is as tasty as others and has very good health benefits. Ragi or Finger millet is very filling and considered one of the healthiest foods, it is rich in calcium and iron.

ITEMS NEEDED
(tsp: teaspoon, tbs: tablespoon, gm: grams, kg: kilo grams, cup: approx. 250ml)

1. Ragi aata (Finger Millet flour) – 1 cup
2. Soya aata / Chawal aata (Soya or Rice Flour) – ¼ cup
3. Pyaaj (Onion) – 1 medium size
4. Hari Mirch (Green Chili) – 3-4 medium size
5. Adrak (Ginger) – 1 tsp (finely chopped)
6. Hara Dhaniya (Coriander Leaves) – 2-3 stems (10-12 leaves)
7. Namak (Salt) – 2 tsp
8. Tel (Oil) – 4-5 tsp

PREPARATION
Finely chop pyaaj, hari mirch, adrak and hara dhaniya.
In a mixing bowl, mix together ragi aata, soya or chawla aata, pyaaj, hari mirch, adrak and hara dhaniya. Add namak and mix well.
Pour water and mix well such that no lumps are formed. Make it into a thin batter.
Heat the tawa or pan and brush it with oil. Pour the batter and spread it slowly in a circular way using the ladle.
Cook it from both sides using oil on all sides.
Serve it hot. Goes well with hari dhaniya chutney.

Recipe 11 :   Chole Bhature - Simple & Tasty

I tried my hands on making the most liked and favourite chole bhature of north. Try this recipe and you may also like the results, my family did. Here we are making a complete dish, chole as well as bhaturas. Putting them as separate recipes seemed a little unfair.

ITEMS NEEDED

(tsp: teaspoon, tbs: tablespoon, gm: grams, kg: kilo grams, cup: approx. 250ml)

For Bhatura (approx. 18 medium size)

1. Maida (White Flour) - 400 gms
2. Cooking Soda – ½ tsp
3. Dahi (Curd) - 100 gms
4. Namak (Salt) - 1 tsp
5. Tel (Oil) - 2 tbs
6. Cheeni (Sugar) – ¼ tsp

For Chole

1. Safed Kabuli Chana (White chickpea)- 250 gms
2. Sabut Garam Masala
    a. Elaichi (Green Cardamom) – 4 pieces
    b. Badi Elaichi (Black Cardamom) – 3 pieces
    c. Tej Patta (Bay leaf) – 1 medium size
    d. Dalchini (Cinnamon sticks) – 3-4 pieces approx. 1 inch long
3. Chai patti (Tea leaves) - 1 tsp
4. Tamatar (Tomatos) - 3-4 medium size
5. Hari Mirch (Green Chilli) - 2-3
6. Pyaaz (Onions) - 4-5 medium size
7. Adrak (Ginger) - 1 inch

8. Dry Masala
    a. Namak (Salt) – 2 tbs
    b. Hing (Asfoetida) – 1 tsp
    c. Jeera (Cumin seeds) – 2 tsp
    d. Lal Mirch powder (Red chilli powder) – 2 tbs
    e. Amchoor (Dry Mango powder) – 1 tbs
    f. Dhaniya powder (Coriander powder) – 1 tbs
    g. Chana Masala (ready-made chole masala) – 2 tbs

PREPARATION

Preparation for this dish begins 8-12 hrs before you intend to make it. In course of making this dish, I have learned a good way to save time. Try to follow the below sequence, hopefully it will help you as well.

First and foremost, soak the chana

Wash the chana and soak them in warm water, to a level that water covers the chana completely. Add 1 tsp of salt and 1 tsp of oil in it. Leave it overnight during winters or around 4-5 hrs in summers. Adding oil will keep the chana intact and its skin will not peel off. Remember to use a big container to soak your chanas as it increases in volume when soaked for a long time.

Now make the dough for bhatura.

Mix maida, soda, salt, sugar, dahi and oil nicely in a kneading bowl. Add warm water slowly and knead the dough. The dough should be soft, softer than what you make for chapati. Knead with soft light hand pressure.

Cover it nicely with a food wrapping sheet or cloth and keep it aside for approx. 8hrs in winters or approx. 4hrs in summers so that it rises well and is ready to be made.

Make the chole first so that they are ready for you to taste with garam (hot) bhatura.

Boil the soaked chana in a cooker or a covered pan with the sabut garam masala; elaichi, badi elaichi, tej patta and dalchini. You can also use the water in which you soaked the chana for boiling. If required add more water so that the chanas are completely immersed. They should be done in 5-6 whistles or 20-25 mins in a covered pan.

Chop the onions and tomatoes into small pieces. Slit the green chillies into two halves length wise. Grate the ginger or cut it in very small pieces.

Now, in a pan or kadhai or deep cooking pot put 3-4 tbs of oil, add hing and fry the zeera. Add onions and fry till they are light brown, then add tomatoes and ginger. Fry the mixture till the tomatoes are soft and all are nicely mixed.

Add the dry masala into it; lal mirch powder, salt, dhaniya powder, chana masala and amchur powder. Mix and cook it nicely till the oil starts separating from the mixture.

Add the fried masala and green chillies in the cooker with the boiled chanas and mix them well. Add 1 cup water, if required and mix it well. Taste the water, add additional salt and lal mirch as per your taste. In case you like your chanas to be a little sour (khatta), add additional 1 tsp amchur.

Do not put the cooker lid, just boil and heat it well on slow flame for another 5-6 minutes.

Now that the chole is getting made, start making the bhatura

Take oil in a pan and heat it well.

Knead the dough softly and roll it into the shape of the bhatura, an oval elongated shape. Sprinkle flour and use little oil for making as the dough is very elastic and not easy to shape.

Put the bhatura in the warm oil. Fry from one side till it rises. To make it rise well, press lightly from where it started rising. Once its light brown, flip the bhatura and fry from the other side.

Serve the Chole and Bhatura's with chopped onions, lemon and achaar (pickle)

Tip: In order to get the black colour in chole, add tea water or wrap the tea leaves in a cloth tightly and put it while boiling.

Recipe 12 :   Bhuna Kathal (Jackfruit) Masala

This is my favourite dish that I love to prepare and eat. In north you generally get the raw jackfruit that is green from outside and white from inside. This is what we will use and not the sweet variety, yellowish in colour that you get in south.

ITEMS NEEDED

(tsp: teaspoon, tbs: tablespoon, gm: grams, kg: kilo grams, cup: approx. 250ml)

1. Kathal (Jackfruit) – ½ kg
2. Pyaaz (Onion) – 5 medium size
3. Tamatar (Tomatoes) – 4 medium size
4. Adrak (Ginger) – 2 tsp (grated or small chopped pieces) or 1inch piece
5. Lahsun (Garlic) – 2 tsp (small chopped pieces) or 5-6 garlic cloves
6. Hari Mirch (Green chili) – 3 medium size
7. Garam Masala powder – 2 tsp (use ready-made or see garam masala recipe)
8. Namak (Salt) – 3-4 tsp
9. Haldi (Turmeric powder) – ½ tsp
10. Lal Mirch (Red chili powder) – 2 tsp
11. Dhaniya powder (Coriander powder) – 1tsp
12. Hara Dhaniya (Green Coriander Leaves) – 2-3 stems
13. Jeera (Cumin Seeds) – ½ tsp
14. Hing (Asfoetida) – 1 tsp
15. Sarson ka Tel (Mustard Oil) – 7-8 tbs
16. Dahi (Curd) – 1 cup

PREPARATION

Start by cutting the kathal (jackfruit) into medium size pieces. Skip this step if you already bought the cut jackfruit.

Before cutting the kathal, grease your hands and knife with mustard oil. This will help as kathal is sticky and might give some irritation in hands later. Remove the green skin and then cut kathal in medium size pieces. Seeds are also edible and has health benefits too, so do not throw them.

Heat oil in a kadai or pan for deep frying. To remove the strong pungent smell of mustard oil, add a pinch of salt while heating. You can see brownish vapours as the oil heats up.

Once the oil becomes light in colour, let it cool down a little. Then on medium flame, deep fry the kathal pieces in the oil till they are brown and become a little crunchy. Keep them aside in a plate.

Tip: Taste a kathal piece to see that it is not bitter. Sometimes the kathal is bitter and the recipe gets spoiled. So, it is better to avoid using it in the dish. Hard luck, get new one to make your dish.

Now to make the masala, finely chop the pyaaz, tamatar, adark, lahsun and hari mirch.

Take another kadai or pan and heat 2-3 tbs of oil on medium flame. Add hing and fry the jeera. Now add the chopped pyaaz and fry it till it is light brown.

Then add adark, lahsun and hari mirch and fry for 1 min.

Add tamatar, mix it well and fry for 2mins.
Now it's time to add namak, haldi, lal mirch, dhaniya powder and garam masala. Mix it well and fry the masala to make a nice paste.

Use additional oil if required in between so that the masala gets cooked nicely and is not sticking to the sides of the utensil. Stir the masala frequently to avoid getting it burned.

You can add some water or dahi ka pani or 1-2 tbs of dahi and avoid using excess oil.

Indication that your masala is cooked is when it has become a good paste and the oil starts separating from the masala. The masala will be concentrated in the centre and oil will be floating over it and along the sides.

Add the dahi and the fried kathal in the masala. Mix them well so that kathal pieces are nicely covered with masala. Taste the masala and if required add additional namak or mirch or garam masala accordingly. Mix well, cover the kadai or pan and cook it on low flame for 8-10mins to let the masala nicely sweep into the kathal pieces. Check on it in between and stir a little.

Ones the kathal masala is cooked, garnish it with hara dhaniya leaves.
Bhuna kathal masala is good to eat with garam (hot) roti or chapati or parathas.

Recipe 13 : Dali Ka Dulha - Khichdi With A Twist

Khichdi is thought of as the meal for the sick, mainly because when it is cooked watery it is light and easily digestible in all conditions. In many north Indian houses, like in my house, it is made lavish with medium consistency, garnished with crispy onion and red chili. Making this dish will be fun with children as well, as we will do some creative work with aata (wheat flour).

ITEMS NEEDED
(tsp: teaspoon, tbs: tablespoon, gm: grams, kg: kilo grams, cup: approx. 250ml)

1. Arhar or Toor Dal (Split pigeon peas) – 1 cup
2. Chawal (Rice) – ½ cup
3. Pyaaz (Onion) – 2 medium size
4. Tamatar (Tomato) – 1 medium size
5. Adrak (Ginger) – 1 tsp (grated or finely chopped)
6. Lahsun (Garlic) – 1 tsp (finely chopped)
7. Hari Mirch (Green chili) – 2 medium size
8. Jeera (Cumin Seeds) – ½ tsp
9. Hing (Asafoetida) – ¼ tsp
10. Namak (Salt) – 2-3 tsp
11. Lal Mirch (Red chili powder) – 1 tsp
12. Gram Masala – ½ tsp (ready-made or see Garam Masala recipe)
13. Aata (wheat flour) – ½ cup
14. Desi ghee (Clarified butter) – 3-4 tsp
15. Paani (Water) – 3-4 cups
16. Tel (oil) – 1 tsp

PREPARATION

Wash and soak the chawal and arhar dal in different containers. You can also use moong dal (petite yellow lentil) instead of arhar dal.

Finely chop 1 onion, tamatar, adrak, lahsun and hari mirch into small pieces. Cut 1 onion into long thin slices.

In a cooker add 2 tsp ghee, hing and fry jeera. Add the chopped pyaaz, adrak, lahsun and fry till light brown. Add tamatar, namak, lal mirch, garam masala and mix it well. Cook for 1-2 mins till tamatar is little soft and mixed well.

Drain the water from the rice and put the rice in the cooker. Mix well and cook it for 1 min.

Drain the water from dal, put the arhar dal in the cooker. Mix well and cook for another 1 min. Now add water, mix well and let it cook on slow flame for 15-20 mins.

In parallel, prepare the dough.

Take the aata in a kneading bowl, add namak and lal mirch. Mix well and knead the dough by slowly adding water. Dough should not be too soft, make it a little hard so that we can make small dumplings. Add oil to dough to make it smooth.
Take small portions and make dumplings of any shape you like, bird, ball, car etc.

Add the dumplings in the cooker with the rice and dal, mix a little. Add more water if required as the aata in dumplings will soak water and we want medium consistency.

Close the cooker lid and put the whistle. Give 2-3 whistles and open the lid only when the pressure inside is completely out.

For garnishing, take a small pan and heat 2 tsp of ghee. Add the kata pyaaz (sliced onion), ½ tsp namak and lal mirch and fry till onion is crispy brown.

Serve the dish and garnish with the crispy onion. Papad, dahi, aachaar are good choices that go well with this dish.

Recipe 14 :   Makhana (Lotus Seeds) Matar

Phool Makhana or lotus seed or fox nut is white, round in shape and resembles popcorn. They are low in cholesterol, fat and sodium and hence are popular as evening snack, tossed in oil or ghee with salt and pepper. They make a good dish with matar (green peas) and goes well with roti or chapati.

ITEMS NEEDED
(tsp: teaspoon, tbs: tablespoon, gm: grams, kg: kilo grams, cup: XXXpprox.. 250ml)

1. Phool Makhana (Lotus Seeds / Fox Nuts) – 1 cup
2. Matar (peas) – ½ cup
3. Pyaaz (Onion) – 1 medium size
4. Tamatar (Tomato) – 1 medium size
5. Hari Mirch (Green chili) – 2 medium size
6. Adrak (Ginder) – ½ tsp (chopped or crushed)
7. Garam Masala – 1 tsp
8. Lal Mirch powder (Red chili powder) – ½ tsp
9. Namak (Salt) – 1 ½ tsp
10. Haldi (Turmeric powder) – ¼ tsp
11. Jeera (Cumin Seeds) – ¼ tsp
12. Ghee (Clarified butter) – 2-3 tbs
13. Hing (Asafoetida) – ¼ tsp

PREPARATION
Wash the green peas or defrost in case you are using the frozen peas. Fresh peas are preferred for a better taste.

Chop pyaaz, tamatar and hari mirch into small pieces. Crush the garlic or cut it into small pieces.

Heat 2 tbs ghee in a kadai, add phool makhanas and ½ tsp namak. Fry them on low heat till they are light brown. Keep them aside in a plate when done.

In the same kadai or pan add 1 tbs of ghee, pinch of hing, jeera and fry. Add adrak and fry a little.

Then add pyaaz and fry till it is light brown in colour.

Now add tamatar, hari mirch, haldi, namak, lal mirch and garam masala and mix it well. Cook for 5 mins. Add ½ cup of water, mix well and on low flame let the masala cook nicely for another 5-10 mins. You will know if the masala is cooked, when the ghee gets separated from it. You can also add milk instead of water for frying the masala.

Once the masala is cooked, add the matar and mix it well.

Cook it for 5-7 mins so that the matar gets soft. Now add the makhanas and mix well. Cook it for another 5-10 mins on low flame.

Garnish it with freshly chopped hara dhaniya (coriander leaves).

Recipe 15 : Chukandar Chana Masala

Chukandar or beetroot is commonly used in salads, adds the rich dark purple colour to the pallete. Beetroot has high iron content and is a good natural blood purifier. Its juice is also pretty common among health freaks. Cooking it with chana or chick peas adds to the flavour and makes a delicious nutritious colourful dish. Chukandar chana masala goes well with roti and chapati or even rice.

ITEMS NEEDED
(tsp: teaspoon, tbs: tablespoon, gm: grams, kg: kilo grams, cup: XXXpprox.. 250ml)

1. Chukandar (Beetroot) – 2 medium size
2. Chana (White Chick peas) – ½ cup
3. Pyaaz (Onion) – 1 medium size
4. Tamatar (Tomato) – 1 small size
5. Hari Mirch (Green chili) – 2 medium size
6. Adrak (Ginder) – ¼ tsp (chopped or crushed)
7. Lahsun (Garlic) – ¼ tsp (chopped)
8. Garam Masala – ½ tsp
9. Lal Mirch powder (Red chili powder) – ½ tsp
10. Namak (Salt) – 1 ½ tsp
11. Haldi (Turmeric powder) – ¼ tsp
12. Jeera (Cumin Seeds) – ¼ tsp
13. Tel (Oil) – 2 tsp
14. Hing (Asafoetida) – ¼ tsp

PREPARATION

Wash the chana and soak them in warm water, to a level that water covers the chana completely. Add ½ tsp of salt and ½ tsp of oil in it. Leave it overnight during winters or around 4-5 hrs in summers. Adding oil will keep the chana intact and its skin will not peel off. Remember to use a big container to soak your chanas as it increases in volume when soaked for a long time.

Boil the soaked chana in a cooker or a covered pan. You can use the water in which you soaked the chana for boiling. If required add more water so that the chanas are completely immersed. They should be done in 5-6 whistles or 20-25 mins in a covered pan.

Peel the skin of chukandar and chop it into small cubes.

Chop pyaaz, tamatar, lahsun and adrak into small pieces. Slit the hari mirch into two halves length wise.

Now, in a kadhai or deep cooking pot put oil, add hing and fry the zeera. Add pyaaz and fry till they are light brown, then add tamatar, adrak and lahsun. Fry the mixture till tamatar is soft and all are nicely mixed.

Add the dry masala into it; lal mirch powder, namak, haldi and garam masala. Mix and cook it nicely till the oil starts separating from the mixture. Add water if required for frying the masala nicely.

Add chukandar and cook it on low flame for 10-15 mins till it is soft. Cover the kadai with lid for fast cooking.

Then add the boiled chanas and mix them well. Add 1 cup water and mix it well. You can also use the water in which you boiled the chana. Taste the water, add additional salt and lal mirch if required. Cook it well on slow flame for another 5-6 minutes so the masala gets seeped into chana and chukandar.

Garnish the dish with fresh and finely chopped hara dhaniya (coriander) leaves. You can also sprinkle pinch of garam masala on top, will give a good aroma.

Recipe 16 : Garam Masala Powder

Garam Masala is one of the key ingredients in north Indian dishes. Generally, people prefer to use garam masala powder but khada garam masala i.e., whole gram masala is also used in dishes like pulao, briyani. Garam Masala is a mixture of grounded spices like dhania, jeera, saunf, elaichi, badi elaichi (black), laung, kali mirch, dalchini, tej patta, jai phal, chakri phool, javitri. These are the most commonly used spices and you can pick any based on your preferences.

ITEMS NEEDED
(tsp: teaspoon, tbs: tablespoon, gm: grams, kg: kilo grams, cup: approx. 250ml)

1. Dhania (Coriander Seeds) – 8 tbs
2. Jeera (Cumin Seeds) – 4 tbs
3. Saunf (Aniseed, Fennel Seed) – 1 tbs
4. Elaichi (Cardamom) – 5 pieces
5. Badi Elaichi (Black Cardamom) – 3 pieces
6. Laung (Cloves) – 1 tbs
7. Chakri Phool (Star Anise) – 1 piece
8. Kali Mirch (Black Pepper) – 1 tbs
9. Dalchini (Cinnamon sticks) – 6-8 pieces approx. 1 inch long
10. Jayphal (Nutmeg) – 1 small piece
11. Javitri (Mace) – 2-3 strands
12. Tej Patta (Bay leaf) – 3-4 medium size dried leaves

PREPARATION
Heat a pan on low flame and add elaichi, black elaichi, laung, chakri phool, kali mirch, dal chini, jayphal, javitri and tej patta. Roast them until they begin to smell good. Keep them aside in a plate.

Now roast dhaniya, saunf and jeera seeds separately and add empty them to a plate. Dhaniya will take a little longer to roast than saunf and jeera will be done quickly.

Let the spices cool down and then add all of them in a mixer. Grind them well to make a fine powder.

Store the garam masala powder in an air-tight container.

Recipe 17 :   Sambhar & Rasam Powder

Homemade sambhar or rasam powder is found in every south Indian home. And why not, when it is easy to make, can be stored for long time and can make it as per one's taste. Rasam and Sambhar powder have the same ingredients except for one that we will see below.

<u>ITEMS NEEDED</u>
(tsp: teaspoon, tbs: tablespoon, gm: grams, kg: kilo grams, cup: approx. 250ml)

1. Lal Mirch Powder (Red chili powder) – 9 cups
2. Dhania Powder (Coriande powder) – 4½ cups
3. Urad dal (white gram) – 1cup
4. Chana dal (Split chickpeas) – 1 cup
5. Arhar or Toor Dal (Split pigeon peas) – 1 cup
6. Kala Sarson (Black Mustard seeds) – ½ cup
7. Kali Mirch (Black Pepper) – ½ cup
8. Jeera (Cumin Seeds)– ½ cup
9. Methi Dana Powder (Fenugreek powder) – ½ tsp

Note: Lal Mirch quantity i.e., 9 is equivalent to the total quantity of 4 ½ (dhaniya powder) + 1 (urad dal) + 1 (chana dal) + 1 (arhar dal) + ½ (kala sarson) + ½ (kali mirch) + ½ (jeera). Remember this ratio in case you want to make less or more.

<u>PREPARATION</u>
Roast urad, chana and arhar dal one by one separately in a kadhai or a pan. Just dry roast them on medium flame till they are light brown. Keep stirring so that they are roasted evenly. Keep them aside in a plate to cool down.

After 10-15 mins, put the roasted dals, kala sarson, kali mirch and jeera in a mixer and grind them to make a fine powder.

Now take a container, add this grounded mixture with dhania powder and mix it well. Then add lal mirch to it and mix well.

Your Rasam powder is ready!

For making Sambhar powder, add methi powder to the above mix.

See how easy it is to make Sambhar and Rasam powder at home. Store them in air tight containers and they will stay good for long time.

Tip: You don't have to make separate Rasam and Sambhar powder. Store Rasam and methi powder separately and whenever you want to make Sambhar, add little methi powder (¼ tsp should be enough to add with 3tsp of rasam powder)

Recipe 18 :   Quick Badaam Kaju Halwa

Halwa is the most common sweet dish that can be made easily and quickly at home. The proportion of ingredients makes all the difference. Halwa needs good amount of ghee, so add ample to make it tasty.

ITEMS NEEDED
(tsp: teaspoon, tbs: tablespoon, gm: grams, kg: kilo grams, cup: approx. 250ml)

1. Suji or Rava (Semolina) – 1 cup
2. Cheeni (Sugar) – 1 cup
3. Ghee (Clarified butter) – 4-5 tbs
4. Kesar (Saffron) – 2-3 strands
5. Kaaju (Cashew nuts) – 10-12 pieces
6. Badaam (Almonds) – 10-12 pieces
7. Elaichi (Cardamom) – 2 pieces
8. Paani (Water) – 4 cups

PREPARATION
Cut kaaju and badam into 3-4 pieces each. Keep them aside, we will use them later.

Take a pan, add water, elaichi and kesar and let it boil on medium flame. Suji and water ratio of 1:4 is preferred i.e., for each cup of suji use four times the water.

In parallel, take a sufficiently big kadhai or a deep heavy pan and heat 4 tbs ghee. Add suji and on low flame fry the suji till it is light brown and you start getting a nice aroma of halwa. You will have to stir it continuously so that the suji is fried evenly and doesn't get burned.

Add cheeni to the suji in the kadhai and mix well. Stirring continuously cook for 1 min.

Generally, the ratio of Suji and Cheeni preferred is 1:1 i.e., for each cup of suji use same amount of sugar. If you like your halwa to be a little sweeter, then add ¼ or ½ cup additional sugar. Be cautious that in case the sugar granules are big then 1 cup may be sufficient. So be careful and based on your sugar variety, adjust the sugar amount. Ratio of 1:1 is safer for most sugar varieties.

Now add the boiled water slowly into the kadhai while continuously stirring so that no granules get formed. Let it boil on low flame for 8-10 mins till the suji is nicely cooked. Water will get absorbed and suji will slightly increase in volume. Pour additional ghee if the halwa is sticking on the sides. You will know that the halwa is done by the sweet smell, aroma and the ghee will start floating on the top.

Now that the halwa is made, fry the badaam and kaju. Take a small pan, heat 1tbs ghee and add the cut kaju and badaam. Fry them till light brown and then add them to the halwa.

Halwa is ready, serve it hot.

Tip: Dry roast suji and store in a container for future use in halwa, upma etc. This will reduce cooking time. Suji will also remain good for longer time.

Recipe 19 : SUIUM – COCONUT JAGGERY BALLS

Suium or coconut jaggery balls is a sweet south Indian dish. Very easy to make with very few ingredients and is fast too.

ITEMS NEEDED
(tsp: teaspoon, tbs: tablespoon, gm: grams, kg: kilo grams, cup: XXXpprox.. 250ml)

1. Nariyal (Coconut) – 1 cup (grated)
2. Gur (Jaggery) – ¾ cup
3. Chawal (Rice) – ½ cup
4. Urad dal (White gram) – ½ cup
5. Namak (Salt) – ½ tsp
6. Elaichi (Cardamom powder) – ¼ tsp
7. Tel (Oil) – 2-3 tbs

PREPARATION

In a mixer, finely grind chawal and urad dal with very little water. It should be of medium flowing consistency.

Pour it out in a container, add salt and mix well. Keep it aside. This will be the coating for the coconut jaggery balls.

Take a kadai or pan and heat gur on low flame till it melts into semi solid form. Add a little water if required.

Add nariyal, elaichi powder and mix well. Cook for 5-8 mins till nariyal is soft and mixed nicely with gur. Keep stirring so that mixture doesn't stick at bottom. The oil from nariyal will start coming out, that's when it is done.

Once done keep the mixture aside to cool down a little. Don't let it cool done completely else it will be difficult to make balls. It should be lukewarm, cool enough for you to hold in hand and make nariyal gur balls.

Grease your hands with oil and make balls of the mixture. Take equal portions to make same size balls.

Heat oil in a kadhai or deep pan on medium flame. Take each coconut jaggery ball, dip it in the chawal dal batter such that a nice coating is formed. Deep fry the coated balls till light brown.

To know that the oil is sufficiently heated for deep fry, put a pinch of chawal dal mixture in the oil. If it comes up quickly and floats on the surface then its ready.

Serve them hot. You can garnish them with badaam or kaju or pista powder or small chunks.

Recipe 20 :   Crispy Meetha Paratha Slices

Few times it so happened that the roti atta (dough) I prepared was a little more, just enough for an extra roti. Storing it for another time didn't seem like a good idea. So, I made mini crispy meetha (sweet) paratha slices. It became a popular sweet dish in my family.

ITEMS NEEDED
(tsp: teaspoon, tbs: tablespoon, gm: grams, kg: kilo grams, cup: XXXapprox. 250ml)

1. Roti Atta (Dough) – enough for a small roti
2. Chini (Sugar) – 1-2 tsp
3. Ghee (clarified Butter) – 2 tsp

PREPARATION

Take the dough and roll out into a thin circle, basically a roti.

Brush the surface of the roti with little ghee. Put cheeni in the centre of the roti.
Fold the roti from all sides to join it at the centre and seal the cheeni inside the round or ball.

With light hands roll out the ball into a circle. Sprinkle wheat flour as required to avoid it sticking to the chakla (surface) or belan (roller). Make it a little thick as there is a filling of cheeni inside. Apply the pressure evenly and gently on all sides.

Heat the tawa or a flat pan and put the cheeni stuffed paratha. Roast the paratha on low flame, cooking it on both the sides with ghee.

Remove it from the tawa when it is nice and crispy. Apply sufficient ghee on all sides for it to be crispy.

After the paratha is made, cut triangular slices like that of a pizza and serve hot.

Useful Tips

Use of Garlic stem in Kitchen

Use the garlic stem while cooking Rajma, Chana, Mutton etc, its helps in cooking them faster

How to Store Lemons

Wipe the lemons dry with a kitchen towel and store them in a glass jar in fridge. They stay good for a long time.

How to keep Green Chilis fresh for 10-15 days

Wash and then dry the chilis. Break or cut the stem of the chili and store them in a dry plastic jar in fridge.

Make Soft Roti or Chapati

Make the dough with milk instead of water. Dough should be soft and kneaded with light hand pressure. Luke warm milk will make it softer. Also, at the end add a little oil (1tsp). Prepare the dough few hours before using to get good results.

Printed in Great Britain
by Amazon

40971887R00031